SEARCHING FOR SHELTER

David Martin Stevens

&

Mardonjon E. Hakimov

KDP

Kindle Direct Publishing

Copyright © 2021 by David Martin Stevens

All rights reserved. No part of this book may be reproduced in any form or by any electronic or mechanical means, including information storage and retrieval systems, without permission in writing from the copyright owner, except by a reviewer who may quote brief passages in a review.

Co-Author of Ghosts in The Mist, Mosque &, The Lighthouse Keeper: Mardonjon E. Hakimov

ISBN 978-1-7365866-1-7 (paperback)

Published by: David Martin Stevens

First Edition
First Edition: February 2021
This paperback edition first published in 2021

To the beautiful and talented souls lost in the dark –
May you find a guiding light in your search for shelter that brings you peace, love, and happiness within these poems

contents

INVISIBLE

For I was not born
of thy same body and mind
broken spirit, character torn
our souls intertwined

For I crave thee
a desire to be one
I accept what will never be
love burned in the light of the sun

I'll stand by your side
watch her cherish what I yearn
swallow my unselfish pride
as my ashes decay in their urn

The weight of my adoration is unsinkable
whilst my illusion drowns and becomes
invisible.........

WHITE CROW

Sunrise; the white crow cries
currents in the rivers flow with hopelessness
streaming about a marred carcass of no purpose

Full sun; the white crow flies
taming the wild wind hunting for happiness
gliding into abyss and ravaged by serpents

Sunset; the white crow dies
thirsting to amuse his ravenousness
starved of validation he submits to malice

THE STAR

He's an actor who dons a delicate mask
shields himself from red roses thrown that die fast
cuts the stems and leaves before he bleeds

He's an actor who doesn't trust the stage
a vulnerability he translates from a scripts page
applause feeds his instinctual needs

He's an actor whose beauty hides in his roots
the scars on his face define a lifetime of abuse
a talent in a theater full of empty dark seats

He's an actor made of porcelain that broke
a manic gentle mind as fragile as a mourning cloak
wears so eloquently a widow's weeds

He's an actor; a victim of romantic tragedy
He's an actor; the star of his own insecurity

WILT

Our innocence crossed paths by happenstance
love blossomed on the bank of a river
we were drawn to each other at first glance
two spring flowers growing old together

I, a handsome and vibrant daffodil
pale yellow and seductively naked
you, a gorgeously perfected tulip
graceful lavender and sweetly fragrant

One by one our petals began to wilt
fresh flowers once alive perish and die
left suffocated by my own self guilt
destroyed our sunlight with no reason why

When the weeping willow casted shadow
an artist painted us like a Van Gogh

LOVE IS HERE TO STAY

Made to be a man to young
taught never to shed a tear
hiding so much pain inside
for all his teenage years

Escape was all he thought about
to live out on his own
but forced he was to live inside
a prison for a home

It's such a lonely world
without someone to care
the bitterness that burns inside
won't get you anywhere

My friend, it's alright
they can't hurt you anymore
get away, get outside
love has opened the door

My friend, it's okay
they can't hit you anymore
no more hate, no more pain
love has opened the door

Struck by things that hurt so bad
the pain will fade away
a friend to share your anger with

Love is here to stay

ASYLUM

Green grass, clear blue sky
mad with anxiety
the lion, sad and shy

Grey clouds, waves in the sea
poisoned humanity
imprisoned, all but free

Brown dirt, lush oak trees
longing for sanity
roots planted, death a tease

White snow, jagged mountains
locked in captivity
eternal, dry fountains

Gold sand, sweltering desert
run from reality
the mind, introvert

One must then inquire
Who might be guilty?
Who is it that is plagued with fire?

Is it this ferocious lion?
Or could it be this beautiful asylum?

I BELIEVED

You thought my ambition was weak
but I knew it to be strong
you thought my dreams were foolish
tried making me believe they were all wrong

When you lost all confidence in me
I believed
When you thought my hopes were too far away to be seen
I believed

Alone in this world
struggling to survive
I needed only myself
to keep my dreams alive

Out on my own
I found the strength to carry on
a force that drove me
far and beyond

When you said I was a failure and could never succeed
I still believed
When you said I was nothing and forced me to leave
I still believed

QUILLS AND FRESH INK

Rhymes impregnated your consciousness
birthed from the tip of your tongue in brilliance
quills embellished the ole parchment page with fresh ink

Poetry flourished loving Jesus
religious prodigy, graceful genius
quills decorated the ole parchment page with fresh ink

Whispers of words preached from the Lords perch
delightful poems immortalized on earth
quills fashioned the ole parchment page with fresh ink

Inspiration from worship and beauty
a poet who wrote fulfilling God's duty
quills made love to the ole parchment page with fresh ink

ALL I HAD

I am scared to realize
I must wake from my dream tonight
for it was wrong to love you
we've shared nothing more than a lie

My vision was weak
I was blinded by deceit

I gave you all I had
honesty, love and more
I'd risk my life to have
your lips kiss me like before

It's so hard to move on
to put you as a memory in my mind
when there is no smile left
to make my sun shine

Perhaps I didn't know you
Did I gaze into a stranger's eye?
I thought I could see so clearly
I believed you were all mine

PROM NIGHT

Little girl
so much to live for
had every dream in the world
her hopes were as high as they could soar
the night had arrived
ready to dance into the spotlight
her breathe they couldn't revive
because the stranger drove drunk
on prom night
April rain brings May flowers
she won't be able to smell them
she just met death within the last hour
no future Romance
the stranger took her only chance
the price is steep the little girl must pay
for a fatal mistake some stranger made
little girl
they buried you today
little girl
your smile
gone forever
far away

HARD CANDY

Tasted so sweet
knocked you off your feet
fed your insatiable appetite
you fell for it at first sight

It loved you in ways
you didn't love yourself
was lost in a maze
trying to find yourself

The clock ticked fast
never escaped your past
you paced the streets in search for hard candy
in your modus operandi

It loved you in ways
you wouldn't love yourself
was lost in a maze
trying to save yourself

You tried to warn me
was too late to see
instead of me, you chose hard candy

Yesterday, you celebrated
your last birthday

POOR MAN

Society suggests
we shouldn't be friends
thou art a black lady
and I a white man

Racial inequality
in tough times like these
thou art a blessed lady
and I a cursed man

You live in the projects
I thrive in a duplex
thou art a rich lady
and I a sad man

Together hand in hand
we share the same land
thou art a wise lady
and I a harsh man

Evolution from slaves
white privilege depraves
thou art a black lady
and I a poor man

BELIEF

God gave me these hands
to hold out to you
god gave me this mind
with the choice to choose

God gave me these feet
to walk down his road
God gave me a soul
never meant to be sold

God gave me this voice
to sing you his love
God made me this man
from his power above

God gave me these brothers
to help in despair
God gave me a choice
to hate or to care

God gave me Jesus
to save me from my sins
God gave me strength
a new chance to begin

Now I'll give back to you
all that you've given to me
your love has set me free
when all that I have
is the belief

DAVID'S FATHER

David's father, he craved to have a son
created three young girls
which he had spoiled each of them with his love

One day his wish came true
but he was unaware
of the secret his wife was trying to hide
the rumors unraveled all her lies

He saw the life he knew for many years Pass him by
everybody admired this man's pride
chose to stay in that unwanted place
and put a happy smile upon his face

Now with a newborn, he held out his two hands
hesitantly accepted him
knowing his son could be another man's

For years to come they'd always feel alone
even more after David had grown
his mother left him there to survive
with a father who blamed him for her lie

David's father was crying alone at night
he never said a word
but they both knew how to hurt each other and fight
his father never realized how lucky he was
when he closed the door
he turned his back on the only son who loved him more

FORGIVENESS

Forgiveness is when someone calls you a name
you still love that person the same

Forgiveness is to give a hug
even to those who don't return your love

Forgiveness is to accept a person for their faults
including if that person broke your heart

Forgiveness is to be there time and again
when you've been pushed away by your friend

Forgiveness is to hold the hand
of someone who's taken the life of another man

Forgiveness is to love your brother
when he hates you for your skin color

Forgiveness is to give the person your food
who has in the past stolen it from you

Forgiveness is to give someone your time
even if that person has cheated you and lied

Forgiveness is to excuse someone for what they don't know
guide and help that person grow

GHOSTS IN THE MIST

At dawn we're spirits that exist
at dusk we become ghosts in the mist
are we living a life predesigned?
or are we making our own path
in a future world already defined?

Our souls were created as one
the weak separated from the strong
never understand our existence
until we are six feet under alive
we ask our creator for forgiveness

We are all sentient beings
feeding our souls distorted feelings
surrounded by glorious nature
we are drawn toward things of material
where more is less and less is greater

Ascend to heaven, descend to hell
caught in between this round wishing well
what is this we're living
on a merry-go-round that keeps spinning
where humanity is what is missing?

BENEATH THE AUTUMN MOON

Beneath the autumn moon
live naked trees
standing tall above their withered leaves
romance filled September air
so crisp, so pure, like a prayer

Pumpkin pies and patches
jack-o-lanterns lit by matches
orchards wrapped with bright red apples

Beneath the autumn moon
kids trick or treat
jammed Halloween bags with sugared sweets
dew drops coat October grass
so clear, so fragile, gently splashed

Turkey leg and wishbones
dried plum atop cinnamon scones
fireplaces made of cobblestone

Beneath the autumn moon
folks celebrate
by grace of God each Thanksgiving plate
harvest blessed November days
the chill, the frost, each moment praised

FLAPPER GIRL

Bobbed hair and fancy lipsticks
divulge her free politics
she beguiles men while smoking her cigarette
rebellious face painted from a painter's palette

She elicits random sex
exhorts men to give her respect
she delineates a self-confident woman
pure imperfection, she's a beautiful human

MOSQUE

Burning steel tumbling from the gates of heaven
nefarious brothers, your sins are forgiven
no day shall erase you from the memory of time
2977 young souls, not ready to die
what you hide in your heart appears in your eyes
a dark shattered world shall emerge into the light

Pray tonight and watch your life change
smile again – may Allah ease your pain
tested was my inner faith
weakness defeated by the gift of his strength

Mosque, a place where I thought I'd never be
Mosque, a place where my creator guided me
Mosque, where I sought new landscapes with new eyes
Mosque, where I learned my old thoughts were wicked lies

I shan't question the journey
because the path travelled
led me here to you

Mosque

SOUVENIR

Narrow, deep and crooked
the longest yet most majestic
she flows uncompassionately, ruffled, brown and swollen
murky beneath her surface, but perpetually hungry
she seduces tortured immaculate auras

An open invitation to bathe
in the beloved untamed
be judicious, for nature can betray the most allegiant
her placidity deceives
while she unleashes a torrent of rage

Auditory sensory silenced
the last breath strangled
H20 can deluge anyone who doesn't fear
and leave a martyr aground as its latest souvenir

LEMON MERINGUE PIE

Mother mixed the egg whites
whipping them vigorously into a frothy,
delectable fluff
light, silky and sweet confection
each beat perfected and pronounced with her affection

Mother's rich buttery pastry
full of smooth and creamy lemon filling
covered with snow cap peaks scorched tawny brown
a tart and sour taste that resonates in the mouth

Oh, how I miss the smell
tantalizing my olfactory system
Oh, how I miss mother's ole fashioned baked pie and its pieces
unable to resist em'

EPISTLE TO THE BLUE PIT VIPER

You slithered into his rainforest
fantastically poisonous
lurking silently 'neath the skin of the sky
the flicker of your tongue beheld him

As with his ancestor's bygone
you lay patiently in wait
stalking him as your prey
starving to ambush his organs and infect his blood

You unleashed your weapon
when he was susceptible and unsuspecting
your fangs punctured his vitality
spewing your toxic venom

Paralyzed pupa
he struggles to break free and fly
it's a battle he fights but will likely lose

He asks you "why is it I you chose?"
eye to eye with elliptical pupils you replied
"your predisposed genetic code"
"for you were meant to suffer my bite"

Dear blue pit viper
learn this and know it well
you may conquer his flesh
but never will you conquer his spirit
not even in death

EVERGREEN

Alive and glistening, thou art the forest
frigid wind blowing and singing a marvelous chorus

Fragrant pine needles cradle white snowflakes
ornaments reminiscent of nature's keepsakes

Winter red cardinals perched upon thy arms
Christmas tree hunters tread quietly sounding an alarm

With each swing of the ax, thou splintered bark cries
a fresh December dawns and begins a new genocide

New Year's will soon arrive in due time
until then my precious evergreen friend
they keep you alive
but only long enough
to rejoice in Christs' life

THE LIGHTHOUSE KEEPER

Beaming blazingly on cheval glass
early morn rays
mirror wrinkles on an old fella's face

Yesterday is his today's memory
tomorrow is his today's dreams
the past increases, the future recedes

Weathered a many storm
rain washed his youth away
stale tobacco decorates his brittle ashtray

Through the endless night
from the lighthouse deck he gives gaze
to the fury of ageless Atlantic Ocean waves

Ships at a distance
their beauty too far to be seen
long past and short future, caught somewhere in between

Having loved and been loved
he reflects to a time back when
a man growing old becomes a child again

FAMILY TREE

Another Christmas eve approaches
nameless red stocking hung from the mantle
gifts under the tree unopened
a nostalgic man weeps next to Christ' candle

No cookies or milk to leave
for a childless dad playing Santa to eat
no sound of pitter-patter small feet
he's alone each Christmas eve

With his mom, dad, and dog
dead and gone
he mourns that he craved only lust
instead of true love

Every twenty fourth of December
he celebrates alone
longing for a child he has never known

Silence defines his Christmas eve
a hollow man grieves
decorating an empty tree

HUSH – HUSH

I said,
Won't you come teach me another tongue?

You said,
Yes, I will bring a book and visit your home tonight.

I said,
Come in. I will learn quickly because I'm young.

You said,
May I touch you in places I like?

I said,
This doesn't feel right. I think you should go.

You said,
My apology, please, nobody mustn't know.

I said,
My dear friend Josephine, Father Mark is secretly gay.

She said,
My young friend Nikolaus, how dare you spread such malicious lies.

I said,
But it's true. He tried to touch me last night.

God said,
My son Nikolaus, be wise. Thy know the truth, and so do I.

A POEM FOR GUILLERMO

He came here with a dream
to make his Mama proud
to be the best man he dared to be
to pursue his goal as he vowed

He risked his life for love
to build her a castle in the sky
that's what his heart is created from
overcame obstacles without a tear to cry

His pockets may have been poor
but his heart was always rich
he struggled everyday
to give all that he could give

A little boy in need
his Mama stood by his side
no money, no food, only ambition to succeed
even when her own dreams had died

Favors can be returned
now her son is by her side
passing years cannot be unturned
but a son's love for his mother shall never die

BLUEBIRDS

Sitting on a branch in an American Holly
two bluebirds chant a song set free from melancholy
they've no fear of the frail perch to break
'tis their wings are the infrastructure of their strength
unearthing the story of each their souls,
reflection on the past
two bluebirds carrying the wounded blue sky,
reflecting on both their backs
merry and feathered, cheery and bright
two bluebirds found peace and happiness together
under one starlight
the most vivid expression of life
two bluebirds painted indigo
flying a distinctive flight
if two happy bluebirds fly beyond a rainbow
to find their pot of gold
let there be hope that love awaits you
and reveals the beautiful secret
between these two bluebirds untold

BORN SILENT

I'll never know you
oh, but how I wish I could
I'll never hug you
the way a brother should

You'll never know me
oh, but how I wish you did
You'll never hold me
with the arms of a kid

Every December
the month you were born silent
we all remember
as we pray for guidance

A crocheted blanket
mommy stitched with love
a white casket
eternal nest for her baby dove

One day we shall meet
when I arrive at the golden gate
and I'll see you smiling so sweet
my brother, my soulmate

TRUMPET BOY

He play's the notes
to an absent audience
everybody knows
he's alone in his own consciousness

Nobody listens...

His only friends
music, bass & treble clefs
high and low notes echoing
in a concert hall full of restlessness

Nobody listens...

Music his only escape
a morose musician who is breathless
a somber melody his horn play's
sings a song about hopelessness

Nobody listens...

The chorus cries heavy
with high notes screaming for acceptance
black dots on paper transposed from the heart
a soloist stumbling into helplessness

But still,
Nobody listens...

ARROW IN HER HEART

She's the onion that doesn't see the knife
She's the day that can't find the night

He's a cloud that drowns her in acid rain
He's a lover that loves to see her in pain

Blind to admit her devotion
Blind to his manipulative emotion

Blind to the spell of his evil art
Blind to the arrow he shot in her heart

DARK MONSTER

The moon cannot shine without darkness
shadows tangle my mind
the wolves howl, the bats fly
so dark, so deep
without darkness
light is incomplete

The horror of dangerous darkness
I get lost in my head
voices scream, words unsaid
ears deaf, blind sight
without darkness
there's no warmth in light

I have unwrapped the curse of darkness
no beacon to guide me
lost in thoughts, deep blue sea
black sky, sad soul
without darkness
fire is blind to charcoal

I stopped looking for monsters underneath my bed
for the only monster to fear in the dark
is the monster alive inside of my head
I don't live in darkness
darkness lives in me

CHENANGO COUNTY FAIR

Hot August nights
candy apples, flavored taffy & fried dough
sold below bright multi-colored carnival lights

Big yellow slide
ticket takers, roller coasters & merry makers
kids being kids enjoying the thrill of each ride

Red tilt-a-whirls
Ferris wheels, cotton candy & house of mirrors
midway games gift cute wins to little boys and girls

Fairground events
country singers, demo derbies & contest drinkers
blue ribbon stock kept hidden under big white tents

Buttered popcorn
miniature ponies, tunnel of love & corn dog cronies
childhood memories naked as the day I was born

SLEEP WELL MY SWEET BABY

When I reached out for a hand
I found your gentle paw
held you tightly in my arms
left your print on my heart

Love is a four-legged word
a home filled with a wet nose
wagging tail and kisses
you fulfilled all my wishes

You never cared about how much money I had
didn't matter if I were handsome, happy, ugly, or sad
no mystery, no deceit
one of the rarest things that is as it seems

You loved kissing my feet and face
you loved me more than yourself
with you in it, the world became a better place
man's best friend, I now must bid you farewell

You have departed from your journey through this life
but will always remain dear to my heart
your spirit flew first class to heaven
sleep well my sweet baby
your unconditional love was a pure blessing

ILLUSORY CALM

Thousands of honey bees swarmed
sweetness in their mouths
stings in their tails
calm minds prevail
I stood still
didn't react
I refused to flail

THE CARPENTER

Master of your craft
carpentry in your blood
passed down from your dad

Hard working rough hands
poor and uneducated
a skilled family man

Harsh life, rarely laughed
sacrificed your smile
for a day's pay to be had

What you built with tools
measured love that never fades
priceless family of jewels

The carpenter built
loyalty and trust
the carpenter built
a home made from sawdust

SNOW GEESE

Well-balanced we will fly as family
Refugees from north seeking southern warmth
Each flapping wing we defy gravity
We flock together through calm and rough
storms

Winter snow approaches as autumn fades
No road is long when united in faith
Teamwork divided builds a stronger strength
We journey thousands of miles in length

Loyalty to those who fall ill and die
We rise together in difficult times
The leader creates lift for those behind
We are a tight convoy well-organized

When one of us falls, the other will fly
Keeping the family strong and alive

THE FIRST SIGN OF THE ZODIAC

I hate it when I can't shut down my brain
I can be up through the night thinking
I hurt more than I will ever show
deeply, silently
but beneath my fiery exterior
I'm a lover who will do anything
and everything for you
I don't know the key to success
but the key to my failure
is trying to please everybody
I have a bad temper
but I don't' stay angry for long
I'm forgiving of people
unless they did something wrong
I'm one of the best person's
you can be friends with
loyal, honest, and trustworthy
I'll always have your back
I don't' love to fight
but I fight for love

EL AMANTE

Dear Amante,

I awoke in the fresh morning hour of 6 a.m.
I recollected a rumination of how lucky I am
our diary composed like a masterpiece
with oil paints, palettes & brushes
each lesson I was vulnerable, impressionable
a callant pupil who new nothing

Like the easel that held my white virgin canvas
I stood erect with my legs spread apart
what we didn't say with words we colored with expression
each stroke of the bristle filbert created our secret story
the passion we painted was without question

If only our masterpiece could survive into eternity
your wife might then see
that art isn't just pigments of paint
but colors of love we paint fearlessly

EARTHWORM

Like an earthworm burrowing through soil
subterranean
its only mission is to reach its destination
dirty and damp
silver and cramped
a melting pot of malady
surface contamination

Steel against steel
the tracks sound a sharp shrill
straphangers swallowing a suicide pill
masks and gloves pretend to protect
but the enemy is awake and potent
circulating, sub rosa
ready to infect

ONE HUNDRED TWENTY ROSES

Bright lights of a dilapidated bordello
mirrored on wet pavement
flickered vehemently, alluring Jon
like a moth to a candle flame

An exquisite enchantress
in a dim lit corridor awaited him
sweetly deceitful
soft flawless cinnamon skin
delicate thin shimmering lips
the Asian masseuse caressed John's chest
with long pink polished finger tips

One hundred twenty roses
with thorns that pricked her coltish hands
aroused Johns weapon of pleasure
like an Olympic champion

Her elegant embroidered dress
fell gracefully to the floor
revealing her ripe, smooth-curved breasts
her lenitive touch hypnotic
a cure like morphine
Jon lay defenseless

From the junction of her thighs
to the heart of her femininity
pools of moisture
collected at the core of her once innocent virginity

COME TOMORROW

Another day, nothing's changed
all these tortured feelings remain the same
my chest trembling like an earthquake
the anxiety exhausting me
I don't know why things are the way they are
or where I will be
come tomorrow

Another day, a lost lamb
I'll never love this weak and broken man
my mind melting like a snow cap
self-doubt poisoning me
I don't know how things are the way they are
or where I will be
come tomorrow

This the last day, I breathe pain
the clouds pass and the sun absorbs the rain
my soul leaving on the next train
dolefulness departing me
I don't know why things are the way they are
the pain will be gone
come tomorrow

I will journey toward the light
and if there's a God
his map will guide me
and I'll accept the reason why things are the way they are
and where I will be
come tomorrow

DIGITAL HEROINE

The human face has become camouflaged
like a soldier of war cloaking himself from the enemy
harmony of colloquy deceased
dexterity of ten digits proficient

Insects under arrest in a spider's web
defiled by the cancer of technology
infatuated with the latest upgrade sensation
the insects thrive like zombies high on digital heroine

I LEFT THE MOUNTAINS BEHIND

I left the mountains behind
to pursue my dreams beyond the countryside
the farms, trees, rivers, and nature
bared their presence
to my youthful eyes

I traded the safe fresh open blue sky
for dangerous congested city life
for yellow taxis driving the streets wild
for tall buildings towering over my inner child

I left the mountains behind
and discovered that the world is unkind
the drugs, crime, greed, and takers
bared their presence
to my naïve eyes

I long to return to where I waved goodbye
for cool evening breezes blowing in July
for yellow buttercups growing in the wild
for one more chance to see those mountains smile

If only I knew then what I know now
with this polluted mind
never – would I have left those mountains behind

DANCING WITH THE BEAST

The gate to the dungeon lifts
opens entryway to the dance floor
the picador on horseback with his decorated banderilla
lances the opponent's player

The matador, his ego center stage
they begin to dance the dance
while the audience cheers for doomsday

El toro is stronger
but the beast is smarter

In the heart of the ballet
el toro returns to querencia
regains his inner strength

The beast is weaker
but el toro is the bleeder

In the deep of tercio de muerte
the muleta attracts the protagonist
the sword torments and tests his endurance
his horn pierces the raw heart, defeating the antagonist

The classic dance complete
el toro takes his final bow

The beast has danced his last dance

STARS AND DREAMS

A little boy looked up toward the sky
he imagined himself as a pilot
saw airplanes and jets flying miles high
through the white crisp clouds where time stood silent

His dream was only a dream to be dreamed
this little poor boy was born on a farm
his dream was too far away to be seen
millions of miles away like a star

Instead, he flew his remote-control craft
as he grew, he saved cash for each lesson
now all I have left is his photograph
my wise uncle George now flies in heaven

So long as a boy imagines his dream
no star is too far away to be seen

WOUNDED SEAGULL BY THE SEA

I was born with wings to soar high
but I fell, weak and wounded
now I crawl through life
living unloved
I'm scared to again fly alone
through an empty sky all on my own

The sorrow cripples my wings
while other seagulls gliding
over the edge of the sea
bask in flight and freedom of loves' glory

To let go of what I desire
is not to deny, but to accept
instead of being confined to the sky
I'm here on the ground
in prison, chained to nature's lie
and I it's inmate, a wounded seagull
unable to fly

YOU

Dropped like a delicate wine glass
my spirit, shattered
never good enough for you
always felt second best, next to you

But I would have flown to the moon for you
sailed every ocean blue for you
climbed the most dangerous mountain for you
if it meant to have just one more millisecond with you

I gazed in the mirror last night and what I saw
was a soul being judged for his gender
a rejected human born with a tragic flaw

I wish I could've been everything you wanted
I wish you could've seen the value in my love
you took for granted

I wish I were pretty and that you would see me differently
I wish for you to find someone to love and to live life blissfully

I just want to escape this body and messed up
dude I grew up to be
he cost me everything that meant most to me,

You

WORDS NEVER DIE

The beat of my core annihilated
light in my eye shadowed by a dark shade
neurons to my brain eradicated

Flesh of my landscape timeworn and decayed
life ticks like a bomb, ends like a grenade

Keeping the love and pain I've lived alive
words in poems I've written will never die

SEARCHING FOR SHELTER

The dawn of the light turned to dusk at night
homeless poor soul abandoned on dark streets
he's floating through the sky like a torn kite
searching for shelter, warm blankets, and sheets

Hot summer days grew cold with seasons change
leaves from maples fell and died as he cried
ice frozen, wandering lost and astray
searching for shelter, dignity, and pride

Dependent on oneself for love and help
makes a poor man less penniless and broke
a man defined by self-worth and not wealth
is a man who found shelter and awoke

The gift of self-love is often unknown
his search for shelter led his rich soul home

About the Authors

David Martin Stevens is an accomplished writer, published poet & SAG actor. He was born and raised in rural upstate New York's Chenango County and currently resides in Brooklyn, NY. He has appeared in several short films, music videos, and has also made a featured appearance on The Tonight Show with Jimmy Fallon in a comedy skit including Ant-Man's Paul Rudd. David enjoys cooking and painting with acrylic's and oil's in his spare time.

Mardonjon E. Hakimov relocated to the United States of America from his native country, Uzbekistan, at a young age. He adapted to his new life where he found a passion for writing in his spare time and has grown intellectually. Mardonjon has already achieved many goals that he set for himself and is inspired in continuing to pursue his future dreams.

www.ingramcontent.com/pod-product-compliance
Lightning Source LLC
LaVergne TN
LVHW041547070426
835507LV00011B/968